iGirl

MY KEEPSAKE

**Fun questions to
tell your story**

This book belongs to:

....

....

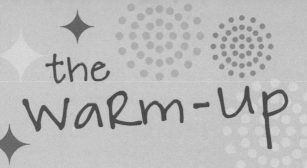

the
WaRm-Up

Full name:...

ORigin of my name:...

My age: ....

My biRthday:..

My mood today:..

The weatheR today:...

Something that made me happy today:..................

Something I am neRvous about: ....

Something I am hopeful about:..............................

The last person I called:.......................................

What I said: ....

Why I am filling out this booK: ....

....

The biggest thing on my mind right now: ....

....

....

me!

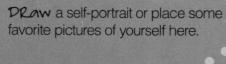

DRaw a self-portrait or place some favorite pictures of yourself here.

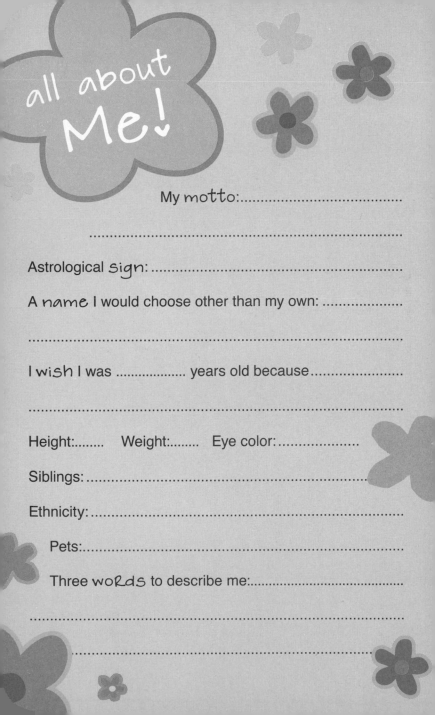

all about Me!

My motto:.......................................

....

Astrological sign: ....

A name I would choose other than my own: ....

....

I wish I was .... years old because.....................

....

Height:........ Weight:........ Eye color:.....................

Siblings: ....

Ethnicity: ....

Pets:..

Three words to describe me:..

....

....

> Your lucky number will always bring you good fortune.

On this date of every month, you will have an amazing day. If you play a sport, make this your jersey number. And if your crush has the same Lucky Number as you, it's a great sign!

Use the chart below to find the numbers that correspond to the letters in your first name and add them up. (Use your birth name, not a nickname.) Add the digits until they become a single digit. For example, the name Isabelle corresponds to 29. 2 + 9 = 11, and 1 + 1 = 2. So if your name was Isabelle, your Lucky Number would be 2!

1	2	3	4	5	6	7	8	9
a	b	c	d	e	f	g	h	i
j	k	l	m	n	o	p	q	r
s	t	u	v	w	x	y	z	

My lucky # is:

....

even more about Me!

What I ate today:...
....

What I had to dRinK today: ....
....

Something I am weaRing right now that I love:...............
....

Something in my backpacK oR puRSe right now:......
....

Something close to me that is smelly:...........................

Song on the Radio right now: ....

Most boRing thing I will do today:...................................
....

Most fun thing I will do today: ....
....

The time I will go to bed tonight: ....

the Fabulous movie of me!

It's time to direct the movie of your life. What kind of movie would it be—romance, action, comedy, drama? Where would it be filmed? What would the movie be called?

Movie Title: ....

Starring (as me!): ....

Co-starring: ....

Supporting Female: ....

Supporting Male: ....

Directed By: ....

Genre: ....

Setting: ....

Synopsis: ....

....

all about
my Family

Favorite Relative:...

Relatives I visit most often:..

....

Relatives I never get to see: ....

Where my grandparents live:...

My parents are...

☐ married   ☐ divorced   ☐ separated   ☐ remarried

How my parents met:...

I most Resemble my...   ☐ father   ☐ mother

What my parents do for a living: ....

....

more about my Family

My relationship with my father is: ....

My relationship with my mother is: ....

My relationship with my sibling(s) is: ....

I am like my mother because: ....

I am unlike her because: ....

I am like my father because: ....

I am unlike him because: ....

Best physical trait I inherited from my mom: ....

Best quality I inherited from my mom: ....

The best physical trait I inherited from my dad: ....

Best quality I inherited from my dad: ....

I am glad my parents taught me: ....

....

....

....

Word list:

- Aunt
- Breakfast
- Dinner
- Goldfish
- Heart
- Kitchen
- Mother
- Nuts
- Sister
- Wacky
- Baby
- Brother
- Dog
- Goodnight
- Holiday
- Laugh
- Movie
- Parakeet
- Thanksgiving
- Bedroom
- Cat
- Family
- Grandma
- Home
- Love
- Nephew
- Present
- Uncle
- Birthday
- Cousin
- Father
- Grandpa
- Hug
- Minivan
- Niece
- Relative
- Vacation

l	f	w	s	e	e	t	a	p	R	e	s	e	n	t
m	o	t	h	e	R	e	h	t	o	R	b	o	e	n
h	u	p	a	R	a	K	e	e	t	e	i	d	h	e
n	h	g	o	o	d	n	i	g	h	t	R	h	c	p
a	h	s	b	R	e	a	K	f	a	s	t	i	t	h
m	o	o	R	d	e	b	e	c	n	i	h	f	i	e
n	w	m	m	g	h	l	a	a	K	s	d	a	K	w
i	a	R	i	e	o	v	a	d	s	o	a	t	a	c
s	c	p	n	n	l	l	m	t	g	e	y	h	t	e
u	K	R	d	v	i	c	d	d	i	n	n	e	R	l
o	y	t	e	n	d	v	n	f	v	v	g	R	a	R
c	y	l	i	m	a	f	a	u	i	t	e	u	e	t
n	c	e	v	n	y	R	R	n	n	s	g	v	h	d
a	c	i	o	h	m	n	g	u	g	h	h	b	o	p
e	R	m	m	e	y	b	a	b	g	b	h	a	a	l

Life at my House

The city and state I live in:...............................

My favorite thing to do in my city: ....

....

The best thing about my house:.......................................

My favorite room in my house:..

A friend's house I like to stay at:.......................................

My favorite memory of having friends over to my house:

....

....

The craziest thing that has happened at my house:......

....

If you opened my fridge, you would find: ....

If I could pick one place to live for a year, it would be: ......

....

my DReam house

Imagine you have a bazillion dollars to build your dream house. How many stories would it have? How many bedrooms? How many bathrooms? Where would you shop to decorate it? What colors would you paint the walls? Would it have carpet or wood floors? DescRibe it!

....
....
....
....
....
....
....
....
....
....

Would it have an indoor swimming pool, grassy lawn, garden, porch, patio…a spa, waterslide, horse stable, rooftop deck, movie theater?!

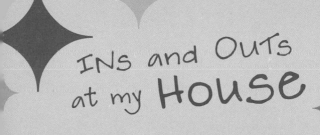

INs and OuTs at my HOUSE

Life at my house is: ....

My favorite thing about my mom: ....

My favorite thing about my dad: ....

How strict are my paRents?

☐ Harsh   ☐ Laid-back   ☐ They don't care

I always get away with: ....

One rule I can't stand: ....

My cuRfew is ....on weeknights and .... on weekends.

The longest I have been gRounded for, and what I did:

....

I love my sibling(s) because: ....

If I am an only child, what do I like about it?........................

....

If I could get another set of paRents, I would choose:

....

Doodle
space

Doodle, scribble, or paste
anything that reminds you of
your family or parents here.

my Fabulous
life at School

My fiRst memory of going to school: ....
....

My current school: ....

GRade I am in: ....

Favorite thing about school:...
....

Least favorite thing about school:...................................
....

Favorite teacheR:...

Least favorite teacheR: ....

Best place to hang out at school: ....

Do I ever ditch class? Why or why not? ....
....

I get mostly ☐ As ☐ Bs ☐ Cs ☐ Ds ☐ Fs

Your favorite color can show a lot about your personality, skills, and what type of career would be great for you. Read on to find out what you could be destined to be!

a colorful CAREER

Blue: You are sensitive, insightful, and believe in creating harmony around you. Be a doctor, nurse, or judge.

Red: You are ambitious, witty, and analytical. Use those skills when you become a lawyer, accountant, or restaurant critic.

Yellow: You are strategic, a good listener, and have a talent for problem-solving. You would enjoy marketing, being a talk show host, or becoming your own boss!

Purple: You are a super communicator with a flair for the artistic and creative side of things. Try advertising or graphic design, or become an artist or musician.

Orange: You are a social person who likes to nurture and help others. Being involved in the community is exciting for you. Be a teacher, flight attendant, or radio personality.

Green: You are level-headed, even in times of crisis. Your loyal, trustworthy nature gives people a sense of security, so you would be perfect as a money-manager, politician, or CEO.

Black: You are determined, outgoing, and enjoy taking risks. You would make a great fashion designer, actor, or journalist.

School
days

Sports I play:..
....

Instruments I play: ....

Clubs I am in: ....

I get detention ☐ weekly ☐ rarely ☐ never

On the weekends, my friends and I like to:...................
....

The last party I went to: ....

A dance I went to and who I went with: ....
....

How I feel about cliques at my school: ....

Am I part of clique? If yes, which one? ....

How people in my school would describe me:.................
....

I think popularity is: ....
....

Most
Likely to...

Make a "Most Likely to" list using the kids in your grade.

Most likely to be a celebrity: ....

Most likely to write a book: ....

Most likely to be a supermodel: ....

Most likely to travel the world: ....

Most likely to be president: ....

Most likely to be a fashion designer: ....

Most likely to be a news anchor: ....

Most likely to win a gold medal at the Olympics: ....

Most likely to be a musician: ....

Most likely to win the Nobel Prize: ....

Most likely to become a detective: ....

Most likely to care for animals: ....

Most likely to have 10 kids: ....

Most likely to work in politics: ....

Most likely to change the world: ....

my Fabulous friends

My best friend: ....

Most important qualities to have in a friend:...................

....

CRaziest thing I've done with my best friend:.................

....

The friend I've known the longest:...................................

A friend who is always there for me: ....

Friend I confide in the most: ....

Friend who gives the best advice: ....

I have bRoKen off a friendship because:..........................

....

Long-lost friend I miss:..

my
FavoRite
fRiends

Write down your best friends' names and what makes you love them. Include a small picture of each friend.

....
(name)

(place photo here)

....
....

....
(name)

(place photo here)

....
....

....
(name)

(place photo here)

....
....

....
(name)

(place photo here)

....
....

my B.F.F.s

The last friend I hung out with and what we did: ....

....

How I greet my friends: ....

Nicknames for my close friends: ....

I get along better with girls/guys because:....................

....

My study friends: ....

My sports friends: ....

My longtime friends: ....

The last fight I had with a friend: ....

A friend I have a crush on: ....

Friend that everyone says I should date: ....

A cool present I got from a friend: ....

My Fabulous Social Life

Start Here

Friday Night:
Party
or
Movie and popcorn

Date with Your Crush:
Double date
or
Solo date

Study for a Test:
Study session with friends
or
Study at home

Hobby:
Gossiping
or
Reading

School Dance:
Dinner with your date
or
Limo with your girls

Best Friends:
Tight-knit group
or
Buds with everyone

Independent Chick:
You don't always follow the pack. You love having time to yourself or getting to know one person really well.

Social Butterfly:
You prefer to be in a group with tons of people around. Staying home? Not an option!

FRiendship Quiz

What Kind of
fRiend aRe you?

1. If a friend wanted to borrow your favorite dress for a party, what would you do?
a. Offer to lend her the shoes and purse that look good with it too.
b. Ask her if you can borrow something of hers and make a trade.
c. Pretend it's at the cleaners—no one can look cuter than you in that dress.

2. The guy your friend has a crush on called and asked you to a school dance. You:
a. Tell him you already have a date, even though you don't.
b. Call her and ask her honest thoughts. Maybe you can all go together as friends.
c. Totally accept—why should you pass up a chance with one of the hottest guys in school?

3. Your friend never does her math homework, and she always asks to copy your answers. You:
a. Hand over your homework.
b. Tell her you'll help her with the problems.
c. Turn her in for cheating. Why should she get credit for your work?

4. You've started hanging out with some popular girls who think your friends are dorks. An old friend walks by while you are eating lunch with the popular girls. You:

a. Wave.
b. Say hi and introduce her to the table.
c. Don't say hi. You'll catch up with her later when you're not busy.

5. You have plans to see a movie with a friend, but then your crush miraculously calls and wants to have a study date. You:

a. Go to the movies and text him the whole time.
b. Curse the world, but ask him for a rain-check.
c. Call your friend and tell her you are going to have to bail on the movies.

Mostly As, Doormat Friend:

You are thoughtful and often go out of your way to help your friends. However, you can be a pushover at times. It's OK to ruffle a few feathers. It will make you better friends!

Mostly Bs, Best Friend:

You recognize that unselfishness, honesty, and compromise make for best friends. Your friends know you always have their backs, so they'll always have yours!

Mostly Cs, Self-Involved Friend:

How can you form great friendships if you're always looking out for yourself? Friendships shouldn't be competitive or one-sided. Try to put your friends' feelings first sometimes, and you will make friends for life.

these are
a few of my
Favorite
things

Food:

Fruit:

Season:

Vegetable:

Ice Cream
Flavor:

Holiday:

Gadget:

Restaurant:

Athlete:

Animal:

Way
to Relax:

Slurpee
Flavor:

my favoRite celebs

Paste magazine cut-outs of your
favorite famous people here.

seeing
staRs

more
FavoRites

TV show: ....

Movie: ....

StoRe in the mall: ....

Guilty pleasuRe: ....

Song: ....

Band: ....

Board game: ....

Room in the house: ....

Magazine: ....

City: ....

Book: ....

Day of the week: ....

Snack: ....

the last Supper

OK, the woRld is ending tomorrow. Draw your last meal, including your beverage and dessert choices.

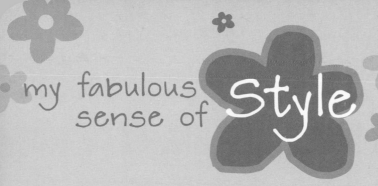

my fabulous sense of Style

Favorite coLoR to wear:...

Favorite aRticle of clothing:..

My paRents hate when I wear: ....

Favorite accessoRy: ....

Last time I got dRessed up:..............................

I am least comfortable wearing: ....

My most sentimental piece of clothing:........................

A clothing tRend I like:...

A clothing tRend I wish would go away: ....

The celebrity's waRdRobe I want: ....

I would describe my style as:

☐ Classic   ☐ Dressy   ☐ Girlie   ☐ Goth

☐ Conservative   ☐ Preppy   ☐ Sporty

☐ Rocker   ☐ Bohemian

my dRЕАм closet

What are your most coveted fashion items? Cut out pictures of your favorite shoes, accessories, bags, dresses, coats, and more, and create a collage of your fashion fantasy.

my CRushes and Loves

My current relationship status:

☐ In a relationship   ☐ Just friends with my crush

☐ Loving the single life   ☐ Looking for love

My first crush was on .... at age ....

I liked him because: ....

....

What happened with my first crush? ....

My favorite thing about the opposite sex: ....

One thing I would change about the opposite sex: .....

....

Physical feature that attracts me the most: ....

....

Non-physical feature that attracts me the most: ....

....

I would never date someone who: ....

Corniest line: ....

build my Perfect Guy

Circle all the qualities, traits, and features that would make up your perfect guy.

Tall	Bookworm	Class clown
Medium height	Talkative	Glasses
Short	Shy	Freckles
Blond	Funny	Baseball hat
Dark hair	Big family	Skateboarder
Curly hair	Only child	Honors classes
Short hair	Likes dogs	Vegetarian
Blue eyes	Sings	Writes poetry
Dark eyes	Big muscles	Cooks
Straight As	Plays an instrument	Good speller
Artistic	Sporty	

MORE
CRUSHES
and Loves

The first person I Kissed: ....

Where did it happen? ....

How I felt afterward: ....

....

My first boyfriend: ....

Who asked who out?..

How long we dated:...

Someone I dumped: ....

....

Someone who broke my heart: ....

....

The best way to get over a breakup: ....

....

Most important thing I have learned about love:..............

....

....

Your Love Personality
palm Reading

A **Heart Line** that starts beneath the index finger represents a normal, healthy love life. You prefer to have a stable boyfriend instead of being single or playing the field.

A line that begins **beneath the middle finger** represents a naïve, materialistic, or shallow view of love. You tend to fall in love easily but often for the wrong reasons.

A line that extends **straight across the palm**, or curves slightly upward, indicates a person who loves unselfishly and gives every relationship their all. You also tend to get your heart broken.

A **short line** across the center of the palm represents a person who lacks interest in love or is hesitant about love. You are independent and generally prefer to be single. In relationships, you tend to be guarded with your feelings.

A **wavy or broken line** indicates a person with many love interests at the same time. You are carefree with love and never have one guy you're too interested in. People probably call you a flirt.

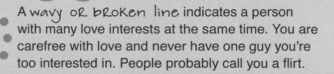

Love is in the air

Do I believe in love at first sight? ....

Have I ever thought I was in love? ....

What I liked about that person: ....

What happened between us? ....

....

Do my parents allow me to date? Why or why not? ......

....

The best thing to do on a date: ....

The best advice I've been given on relationships:...........

....

My current crush: ....

If I could tell him one thing, it would be:..........................

Does he like me too? ....

With my crush, I am hoping:...

....

my cuRRent CRush

On a separate piece of paper, write down the name of your biggest cRush, why you like him, and today's date. Then fold it up and tape it to this page. In a few months, open it and see how you feel about him. Who knows, maybe he'll be your boyfriend!

date:

My cuRRent cRush

Top Secret

Do Not Open

my QUIRKS and IRKS

My quirkiest talent:..

....

A talent no one knows about: ....

....

An odd pastime of mine: ....

....

Weird thing that makes me laugh: ....

....

Weird foods I love to eat:.......................................

A quirk I have about food: ....

....

One word I always say:..

....

Phrase I always say: ....

....

....

Supergirl

Now imagine you're a **superhero**. Draw yourself. What are your powers? What do you call yourself?

Every girl has quirky special talents

My Superhero Name

more QUIRKS and IRKS

My quirkiest physical feature:.....................................

Unexpected feature I'm attracted to:.............................

Weirdest collection: ....

....

Most bizarre item in my house:.....................................

....

Habit my friends would think is strange:.........................

....

Person I secretly idolize:..

....

Normal thing other people can do that I can't do:...........

....

Dumbest TV show I still like: ....

Silly song I still like: ....

Write down a weird or crazy dream you have had. Use this Dream Decoder to make sense of it!

....
....
....
....
....

my
DReam
DecodeR

Baby: You are nervous about a situation and aren't sure how to handle it.

Monkey: Someone you know is trying to deceive you—watch out.

FiRe: An important change or transformation is coming!

StoRm: You are struggling with shock or a sudden loss.

Flying: You must let go of trouble weighing you down, such as a breakup.

Bees: Good luck is coming your way!

Teeth falling out: Bad news is coming or you may be about to fail at something.

BiRd: Stability and security are coming your way.

Kissing: You have affection for someone, but aren't sure how to show it.

FloweRs: A friend needs your help or compassion.

coLoR blue: Someone needs your loyalty.

Running: You did something hurtful or wrong and need to own up to your actions.

ShaRk: You are feeling bitter or angry about something and need to resolve it.

coLoR fuchsia oR puRpLe: You are ready for a new attitude!

coLoR gold: Money and riches are in your future!

my Travels and Adventures

My favorite vacation: ....

Favorite city I've visited, and why: ....

....

Favorite country I've visited: ....

Somewhere I'm interested in visiting, and why:..........

....

Number of states I've traveled to: ....

Most exotic place I've traveled to: ....

Foreign city I'd like to live in: ....

Favorite beach vacation: ....

Favorite winter vacation: ....

....

Favorite Road trip:..

....

Stick pictures, maps, tickets, souvenirs, and other mementos from your favorite vacation of all time on this page.

the woRld's greatest vacation

Out and About

My most Relaxing vacation:..

Nightmare vacation:..

The best thing about being on vacation:...........................

A trip I took with friends: ....

Most fun activity I did while on vacation:...........................

Coolest landmark I have visited: ....

My next trip will be: ....

I would like to...

☐ ride horses on the beach   ☐ see the Eiffel Tower

☐ bungee jump   ☐ ride jet skis

☐ swim with sharks   ☐ sleep on a houseboat

☐ climb Mt. Everest   ☐ go to the top of the
                                   Empire State Building

☐ scuba dive

☐ hike the Great Wall   ☐ hike a volcano
    of China

                           ☐ tour the rainforest

☐ sail a boat   ☐ ski the Swiss Alps

☐ ride in a hot air balloon   ☐ ride an elephant

☐ explore a cave

Where would you go on your dream vacation? Who would you invite to go with you? Describe your ultimate vacation.

my DReam vacation

My ItineRaRy

....

....

....

....

....

....

Sending You a Postcard

Paste a picture of your
dream vacation spot here.

This or That?

Circle the "This" or "That" you like best.

blond	-or-	brunette	waffles -or- pancakes	
black	-or-	white	basement -or- attic	
apples	-or-	bananas	SUV -or- sports car	
mountains	-or-	beach	brains -or- beauty	
dogs	-or-	cats	gold -or- silver	
morning	-or-	night	deep -or- shallow	
popcorn	-or-	candy	hate job/ make lots of money -or- love job/ make a little money	
heels	-or-	flip-flops		
hug	-or-	handshake	jeans -or- dress	
pen	-or-	pencil	inside -or- outside	
summer	-or-	winter	baseball -or- football	
rap	-or-	country	swimming -or- skiing	
very tall	-or-	very short	odd -or- even	
meat	-or-	veggies	fly -or- drive	

This OR That?

Circle the "This" OR "That" you like best.

Mac -or- PC

skydiving -or- bungee jumping

Chinese food -or- Mexican food

book smarts -or- street smarts

Zac Efron -or- Justin Bieber

spring -or- fall

East Coast -or- West Coast

fast -or- slow

cake -or- pie

tame -or- wild

stripes -or- dots

hot cocoa -or- tea

sing -or- dance

TV -or- computer

antique -or- modern

surf -or- skate

creamy -or- crunchy

sunshine -or- rain

weird -or- normal

piercing -or- tattoo

half-empty -or- half-full

fiction -or- nonfiction

ice cream -or- frozen yogurt

milk chocolate -or- dark chocolate

airplane -or- sailboat

have I EVER?

Raked leaves ☐

Eaten a bug ☐

Ditched school ☐

Been in a car accident ☐

Jumped on a trampoline ☐

Thrown water balloons ☐

Acted in a play ☐

Talked with a therapist ☐

Flown in a helicopter ☐

Been in the newspaper ☐

Sung karaoke ☐

Won an award ☐

Gone down a waterslide ☐

Snorkeled ☐

Made a snow angel ☐

Entered a beauty pageant ☐

Eaten rabbit ☐

Driven a car ☐

Won a contest ☐

Been on a reality TV show ☐

Drank coffee ☐

Traveled alone ☐

Thrown a surprise party ☐

Gotten in trouble at school ☐

Lost a bet ☐

Made ice cream ☐

Had surgery ☐

Started a food fight ☐

been there, Done That

Won a spelling bee ❏

Been in a bowling league ❏

Gone rock climbing ❏

Ridden a horse ❏

Spoken in more than
one language ❏

Seen a ghost ❏

Gotten detention ❏

Written a poem ❏

Been scared of the dark ❏

Invented something ❏

Swam with dolphins ❏

Been to the circus ❏

Traveled to Europe ❏

Played Spin the Bottle ❏

Been to a wedding ❏

Gotten an F ❏

Been to a school dance ❏

Seen the movie
Dirty Dancing ❏

Done a backflip ❏

Built a snowman ❏

Wet the bed ❏

Taken a ballet,
jazz, or tap class ❏

Been white-water
rafting ❏

Received a dozen roses ❏

Caught a ladybug ❏

Tricky
Situations

What would I do...

If I found a wallet with $100 in it, would I keep it? ....

If I was marooned on a deserted island, who would I bring?...

If I had to eat only one food for the rest of my life what would it be?..

If I saw my friend's significant other kiss someone else, what would I do?...

If I found my best friend's diary, would I read it? ....

If I could turn invisible would I use my powers for good or evil? ....

If I found the answers to a test, would I look? ....

If I was grounded but wanted to go to a party, would I sneak out? ....

If a teacher had toilet paper stuck to her shoe, would I tell her?...

in a
Pickle

Describe the **toughest** situation you have ever had to deal with and what you did.

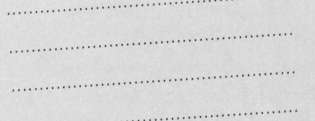

my Fears

My biggest fear:...
....

IRRational fear I have:...

Biggest fear as a child:...

Fears I have oveRcome: ....

....

even fab girls can be afRaid sometimes...

Fear about myself:.......................
....

....

Fear for the futuRe:..

Fear about school:..

Fear about love: ....

Fear about maRRiage:...

Fear about paRenting:...

....

....

....

a very
SCARY
day

Describe a situation that
completely FReAKeD
you out. What happened,
and how did you react?

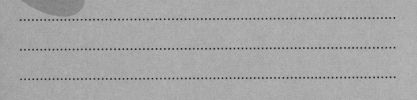

....

....

....

....

....

....

....

....

....

....

....

....

....

....

....

What am I Afraid of?

Dream that made me wake up in a cold sweat: ....

....

Fear about failure: ....

My greatest fear for the country: ....

....

My greatest fear for the environment: ....

....

My greatest fear for the world: ....

....

Fear about growing up: ....

....

An authority figure I fear: ....

Fear about natural disasters: ....

Fear about death: ....

my fear-o Meter

On a scale of 1-10,
how much does this
stuff scare you?

spiders ....

heights ....

sharks ....

the dark ....

water ....

flying ....

snakes ....

thunder ....

speaking in front
of the class ....

falling down

the stairs ....

not being liked ....

getting dumped ....

needles ....

being trapped
in a small space ....

sharp knives ....

roller coasters ....

war ....

balloons popping ....

pants falling down ....

tornadoes ....

drowning ....

my fabulous Fantasy world

One feature I'd change:..

Celebrity I'd marry:..

Movie I wish I was in:..

One thing I wish I had invented:..................................

If I could fly, I would go: ....

....

If I could teleport to one place in the world:...............

If I won the Lottery, the first thing I would do:.............

....

If I could be the other sex for one day:.......................

If money were no object, I would:................................

If I was an animal, I would be:....................................

If I was a flower, I would be:.......................................

If I could be one element of nature: ....

who's coming to Dinner?

If you could invite three people, dead or alive, to have a dinner party at your house, who would they be and why?

PeRson 1

PeRson 2

PeRson 3

in my dream
WoRld

If I could take back one thing from my life, it would be: ....

....

If I could time-travel, I would:.......................................

....

If I could make one person fall in love with me:..................

....

If I was invisible, I would: ....

One food I would eat for the rest of my life: ....

One disgusting food I'd wipe off the planet:...................

If I could walk through walls: ....

If I was an Olympic athlete in one sport: ....

If given the choice, I would be a:

☐ model   ☐ pro athlete

☐ actor   ☐ Nobel Prize winner

☐ rock star   ☐ CEO of a large company

☐ musician   ☐ the President of the United States

Genie in a Bottle

Poof! A genie suddenly appears and grants you three wishes! What do you wish for?

Wish 1: ....

....

....

....

Wish 2: ....

....

....

....

Wish 3: ....

....

....

....

my many Moods

SCARED:

The last time I felt...

Amazing:..

Irritated: ....

Anxious:..

Guilty: ....

Loved: Bored: ....

Blissful: ....

Jealous: ....

Hopeful:..

Embarrassed: ....

Nostalgic: ....

CReative:

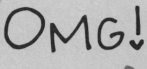

OMG!

What is your most mortifying, embaRRassing moment ever? Rate it on a scale of 1-10.

....

....

....

....

....

....

....

....

....

....

....

....

Rate My OMG
Moment:

More of my many Moods

The last time I felt...

Comfortable: ....

Lonely: ....

Depressed: ....

Beautiful:

Paranoid: ....

Surprised: ....

Stressed: ....

Respected: ....

Satisfied: ....

Confused: ....

Confident: ....

Mischievous: ....

Inspired: ....

Me
today

Write down how you're
feeling or whatever is
on your mind today...

....
....
....
....
....
....
....
....
....
....
....
....

My mood: ....

my Playlist

Music I listen to when I am...

Bummed out: ....

Getting ready for a party: ....

Hanging out with friends: ....

Feeling creative: ....

Cleaning my Room: ....

Sleepy: ....

In love: ....

Studying: ....

Getting over a breakup: ....

Relaxing: ....

Depressed: ....

Exercising: ....

In a silly mood: ....

Dancing in front of the mirror: ....

Quote
garden

Write down your faVoRite quotes.

life quote:

"   "

friend quote:

"   "

love quote:

"   "

.... quote:

"   "

my

Top 3

Things I want to *accomplish* before I am 100: ....

....

Things I need to be *happy*: ....

....

Qualities I need in a *boyfriend*: ....

....

Qualities I need in a *friend*: ....

....

Things I'd take to a deserted *island*: ....

....

Important *people* in my life: ....

....

Things I am *grateful* for: ....

....

....

....

Looking
back

Stick photos from
your best memories here.

three Things

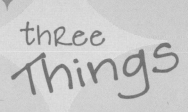

Guilty pleasures: ....

....

Things to do on a Rainy day: ....

Things to do on a summer day: ....

Splurges: ....

Unforgettable moments in my life: ....

....

Possessions I'd save in a fire:........................

....

Things that inspire me: ....

....

....

Things I would tell my past self if I had a chance:

....

....

....

Stick photos of you with the top three most important people or things in your life here.

three
Best

my Year
at a glance

Coolest place I went:...

....

Things I learned about myself this past year:...............

....

....

Time I felt most creative:...

....

My biggest obstacle this past year:...............................

....

Most drastic change:...

....

One thing from the year I would take back:......................

....

My most difficult task of this year: ....

....

a Note from Me

Write a note to a person who was significant (good or bad) during the past year.

....
....
....
....
....
....
....
....
....
....
....
....
....
....
....

My goal for the upcoming year:..

....

I believe the secret to my future happiness is:...............

....

After high school, I hope to:...

An adventure I plan to go on: ....

If I do not get married, I feel like I will be missing out.

☐ Yes   ☐ No

Marriage is a/n .... thought for me.

I want .... Kids; .... boys and ....girls.

Names I like for kids: ....

Where would I like to be living in 5 years, and why:.........

....

A friend I know will always be in my life:..........................

A skill I'd like to develop:...

my Will

If I die tomorrow, I hope it happens while I am ....

.... I will miss ....,

...., and ....

the most when I am gone. One thing I am NOT going to

miss is...

I leave my clothes and shoes to ....

I leave my makeup to .... I leave

my favorite purse to..................................... I leave my

jewelry to .... I leave my favorite

CDs and DVDs to .... I leave

my pet/s to .... I designate ....

.... to look after my boyfriend/crush. I will hide

this journal in .... and only tell ....

...............................the location. I would like to be buried in

...........................while wearing ....

....

more
Hopes
and Dreams

A foRtune I'd like to find in my fortune cookie: ....

A RisK I want to take:..

A tRadition I'd like to keep in coming years: ....

My dream job would be:...

In 10 years, I picture myself:..

In 50 years, I picture myself:..

One thing I will be disappointed if I don't accomplish:...

....

One person I would like to meet, and why: ....

....

Why I love being me!...

....

....

Gratitude Diary

Make a list of all the things—big and small—that you are grateful for! Add to it anytime you like.

....
....
....
....
....
....
....
....
....
....
....
....
....

being you IS fabulous!

B.F.F. Quizzes

FREE APP!

Take & create unlimited quizzes!

Share via Facebook & Twitter!

Visit BFFquizzes.com for more info